Have You Snuzzled a Wuzzle Today?

By Emma E. Dunlop
Illustrated by Pat Paris

Random House 🏠 New York

Library of Congress Cataloging in Publication Data: Dunlop, Emma E. Have you snuzzled a Wuzzle today? SUMMARY: A collection of poems about the magical Land of Wuz and its inhabitants.   1. Children's poetry, American.   [1. American poetry]   I. Title.   PS3554.U46977H3   1985   811'.54   85-2141 ISBN: 0-394-87495-1

Manufactured in the United States of America   1 2 3 4 5 6 7 8 9 0

The Land of Wuz

The Land of Wuz is magical,
The grass is always green,
Spring is always in the air,
And winter's never seen.
Apples, pears, and apricots
Drop lightly from the trees
While birds and bees and butterflies
Delight in every breeze.

The land of Wuz is bright and clear,
There's never any gloom,
And when it rains, it's just enough
To help the flowers bloom.
To visit this enchanting land,
There's something you must do—
Snuzzle a Wuzzle a little while,
And Wuz will welcome you.

Butterbear

There's a very special Wuzzle
Made of golden velvet fur.
She loves to talk to flowers,
And they love to talk to her.

Her wings are pink and delicate;
They're like a butterfly's.
She cares a lot for others,
You can see it in her eyes.

She is soft and tenderhearted,
When she's needed, she is there.
You will always feel much better
When you snuzzle Butterbear.

Moosel's Happy Sea Song

I love to swim all morning
In the billows of the sea.
I wave to all the fishes
As they come to play with me.

It's fun to flap my flippers
On a sunny afternoon
As I dive beneath the water
Of our beautiful lagoon.

I'm happy every evening
When I frolic in the foam,
Then swim back to my island
And my little lighthouse home.

Bumblelion

Three cheers, three cheers for Bumblelion,
The Wuzzle king of sport;
He's first upon the playing field
For games of every sort.
He's stronger than a lion
And he's swifter than a bee;
He loves to run, he loves to jump,
He loves to swim and ski.

Three cheers, three cheers for Bumblelion,
He's merry and he's brave,
And should he happen not to win,
He does not misbehave,
For he believes in sportsmanship,
It fills him to the brim.
So shout "Hoorah!" for Bumblelion,
Three cheers, three cheers for him.

Hoppopotamus

The snuzzly Hoppopotamus
Is dancing through the air.
She's rather large and clumsy,
But she does not seem to care.
She thinks that she is dainty
And believes that she has grace,
So she's never fazed the slightest
When she falls upon her face.

The snuzzly Hoppopotamus
Eats far more than she should.
She sometimes tries to diet,
But it doesn't do much good.
Yet she knows it doesn't matter
If she never sheds an ounce,
For she likes herself already,
And that's all that really counts.

Eleroo

Eleroo is a wonderful Wuzzle
Who collects every manner of junk.
He frequently searches for bargains,
Which he carefully sorts with his trunk.
His house is crammed clear to the rafters
With treasures he'll never throw out.
He has dozens of broken alarm clocks
And a teapot that hasn't a spout.

He's a very creative inventor
And has always got some new device.
His pouch holds a hammer that whistles
And a yo-yo that yodels to mice.
If you'd like a wind-up banana,
Or a lantern that serves as a shoe,
Then snuzzle this wonderful Wuzzle—
Eleroo is the Wuzzle for you.

Rhinokey's Puzzle Song

I'm a puzzle of a Wuzzle,
I behave the way I please,
And I find it very pleasing
To bamboozle and to tease.
I may make you very sneezy
With some powder in your nose;
I may spray you with the nozzle
Of the nearest garden hose.

I'm a Wuzzle who is busy
Being dizzy every day,
Wearing dozens to a frazzle
With the crazy tricks I play.
Though some other Wuzzles sizzle
When I'm on a zany spree,
I will never trick or tease you
If you'll only snuzzle me.

AcHOOoo

Moosel's Fix-it Song

When your blender isn't blending,
And your banjo's on the blink,
I can mend them in a minute,
In a second, in a wink.

If your camera is not snapping,
And your toaster's lost its pop,
I will quickly have them clicking
In my little fix-it shop.

Here I'll fix your feather duster
And adjust your old TV,
Anything you've got that's busted—
Just bring it here to me.

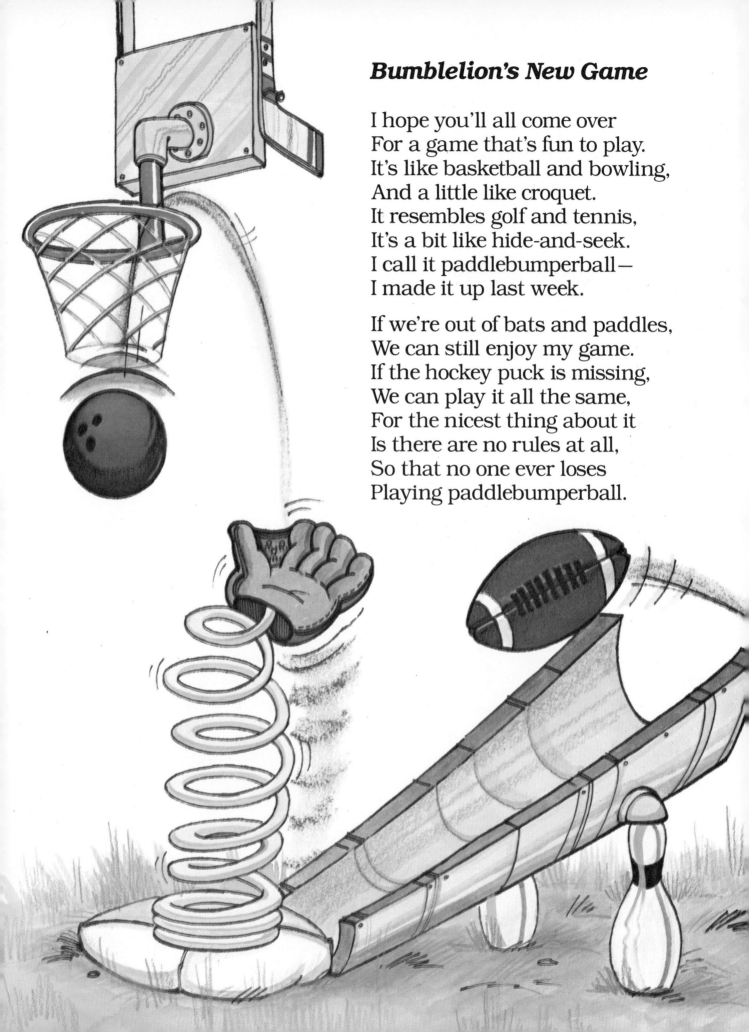

Bumblelion's New Game

I hope you'll all come over
For a game that's fun to play.
It's like basketball and bowling,
And a little like croquet.
It resembles golf and tennis,
It's a bit like hide-and-seek.
I call it paddlebumperball—
I made it up last week.

If we're out of bats and paddles,
We can still enjoy my game.
If the hockey puck is missing,
We can play it all the same,
For the nicest thing about it
Is there are no rules at all,
So that no one ever loses
Playing paddlebumperball.

BAM

Rhinokey's Picnic

At Rhinokey's latest picnic
At his private picnic spot,
All the Wuzzles came with baskets,
All the Wuzzles ate a lot.
They brought bowls of parsley pudding
And bananaberry stew;
There was raisin radish salad
That was difficult to chew.

There were plates of pickled peanuts,
There were lemon onion pies,
A dish of cabbage custard,
And some spinach squash surprise.
Then Rhinokey served a portion
Of a food that has no name.
All the Wuzzles loved the picnic
And were very glad they came.

Eleroo's Invitation

My limousine is waiting.
Won't you join me for a ride?
It's painted and it's polished.
There is room for you inside.
I made it just this morning.
It's an up-to-date machine
That runs on clocks and zippers,
So it needs no gasoline.

It's built of bowls and bumbershoots,
Of bells and shells and shears,
Assorted spoons and showerheads
I'd saved for years and years.
I hope you'll sit beside me
And survey the passing scene
From my brand-new, beautiful, one-of-a-kind
Luxurious limousine.

Butterbear's Flower Song

Good morning, azalea,
Hello, buttercup,
Awaken, carnation,
It's time to get up.
The stars have all gone,
And the sky's turning blue.
I'm glad to be singing
Good morning to you.

Arise, drowsy daisy,
Sweet lilac and rose,
The day is no time
For a blossom to doze.
Open your petals
In lovely display
And join me in greeting
This glorious day.

Hoppopotamus's Tea Party

Do join me today
For some beanberry tea.
We'll sit in the shade
Of the appleplum tree,
And there as we sit
Sipping tea in the shade,
I'll serve you a tray
Of some tarts that I made.

I'm sure you'll enjoy them,
They're pearpepper tarts,
Extremely delicious,
And shaped just like hearts,
And when we have eaten
Two hundred and two,
I'll be very happy
To dance just for you.

Snuzzle a Wuzzle Today

Wuzzles are cuddly companions
With hearts that are warmer than toast,
Friends you can always depend on,
Whenever you need them the most.

No matter how sad you are feeling,
Your Wuzzle will soon make you smile.
You're sure to feel better in no time
When you snuzzle your Wuzzle awhile.

Your Wuzzle is always there waiting
To help make your cares go away,
So snuggle up close to your Wuzzle,
And snuzzle your Wuzzle today.